Italian Christmas Eve: The Feast of Seven Fishes

Linda and Rocco Maniscalco
Illustrations by Linda Maniscalco

A Reminiscence with Recipes

© 2010 by StataBuon.com
Italian Christmas Eve: The Feast of the Seven Fishes
A Reminiscence with Recipes
Written by Linda and Rocco Maniscalco
Illustrated by Linda Maniscalco

All rights reserved. No part of this publication may be reproduced or transmitted in any form or by any means, electronic or mechanical, including photocopy, recording or by any information storage and retrieval system, without permission in writing from the publisher.

First published in the United States of America in 2010 by StataBuon.com
ISBN: 978-0-615-40881-1
First Edition
Library of Congress Control Number: 2010915302
Printed in U.S.A.

Cover design by Mary Venditta

Stata Buon

In these authentic Italian recipes passed from one generation to the next, home cook Linda Maniscalco and her husband Rocco, a master mixologist, explain step-by-step how to create the Feast of Seven Fishes. Since Advent is a penitential season in which devout Italians abstain from rich foods in preparation for the coming of Christ, the Feast of Seven Fishes is a delicious, healthy way for today's Italian-American families to celebrate their heritage.

"Stata buon" is an Italian toast that means "staying well." Join us in reclaiming the family traditions of our Italian ancestors, and create a simpler way of life, if only for one special night. "Stata buon" is good for the body as well as the soul.

The Season of Advent

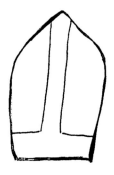

The word "advent," from the Latin adventus, means "coming" or "arrival." The liturgical season of Advent is focused on the "coming" of Jesus as Messiah, both in His birth at Christmas and in His future second coming. This is why the Scripture readings during Advent include both Old Testament passages related to the expected Messiah, and the New Testament passages concerning Jesus' second coming as judge of all people. Also, passages about John the Baptist, the precursor who prepared the way for the Messiah, are read. All of these themes are present in Catholic worship during Advent, which the Catechism of the Catholic Church succinctly describes:

> When the Church celebrates the liturgy of Advent each year, she makes present this ancient expectancy of the Messiah, for by sharing in the long preparation for the Savior's first coming, the faithful renew their ardent desire for his second coming. By celebrating the precursor's birth and martyrdom, the Church unites herself to his desire: "He must increase, but I must decrease" (524).

Advent is not part of the Christmas season itself, but a preparation for it. Thus, Catholics do not sing Christmas hymns, or use Christmas readings in Mass until December 25th, the first day of the Christmas season. The character of worship during Advent is more solemn, quiet, and less festive than during other times of the year. In the Catholic Church, for example, the Gloria in Excelsis is not used. As Caryll Houselander writes in her famous spiritual book on the Blessed Mother, *The Reed of God*, "Advent is the season of the secret, the secret of the growth of Christ, of divine love growing in silence. It is the season of humility, silence, and growth."

–The Most Reverend John O. Barres, S.T.D., J.C.L., D.D.
Bishop of Allentown

A Typical Italian Christmas Eve

The custom of most Italian families on Christmas Eve is to have a big dinner early in the evening and then later go to the Midnight Mass. In preparation for the dinner, the mother starts to cook early in the morning and by the evening, the house is filled with wonderful Christmas aromas. Some of these foods are prepared and eaten only once a year, making this dinner and this night so very special.

We might say that the seven fishes represent the seven sacraments. In the Hebrew culture, the number seven is the perfect number. The seven fishes are food for the body, the seven sacraments are food for the soul.

This dinner is truly unique because we celebrate the preparation for the greatest birth that ever happened—God Incarnate!

– Rev. Monsignor Felix A. Losito
  Holy Rosary Church, Reading, Pennsylvania

This book is dedicated to our children
Adam, Katrina and Gabriella
—and—
In memory of our family who taught us love:
Benjamin Maniscalco, Jr., Ann Cicero Maniscalco,
Joseph Pitarra, Anthony Pitarra, Mary Nardone, Anna Savarese,
Rose Curry, Clara Struzzeri and Josephine Caggiano Maniscalco

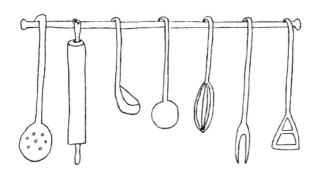

Advent 8
Feast of the Seven Fishes 9
Salt Cod (Baccala) 10
Octopus (Polpo) 12
Anchovies 13
Eel 15
Squid (Calamari) 17
Cuttlefish (Seppia) 18
Smelts 20
Seafood Stew (Cioppino) 21
Antipasto & Vegetables 23
Midnight Mass 29
Cookie Exchange 30
Chestnuts 38
Beverages 40
Where to Shop 44
Index 46
Acknowledgments 48

Advent

For most Italian Americans, the season of Advent—the four weeks leading up to Christmas—is special. As if preparing for the actual birth of a baby, the family runs about in a flurry of activity, getting ready for the arrival of the Christ child.

The Italian home, always kept spotless, is scrubbed even cleaner in anticipation of the Christ child. My father would say, "Your mother and her sisters, they clean-and-a-cook like-a-crazy!" Nonna Christina said in Italy every household, even the poorest, puts out its best during Advent. The woman cooks. Children are sent outdoors to gather greenery for decorating. The family makes an Advent wreath of greens and candles, three purple and one pink. One candle is lit each Sunday to mark the passage of the weeks of Advent.

Since Advent is a penitential season, many devout Italians abstain from meat and sweets as they prepare for the coming of the Savior. All the cooking, cleaning and candle-lighting culminate on Christmas Eve in the Feast of Seven Fishes—the grandest fast of all. According to tradition, Christ hasn't been born yet when the feast takes place, so this food sets the stage for the nighttime vigil (La Viglia) known as Christmas Eve Mass.

The celebration of Christmas is important to Italians not because of gifts or Santa, but because it marks the birth of Jesus Christ, who is at the center of our Catholic belief. A nativity scene is displayed in every household that can afford one, and the Christ child is placed in the manger after midnight Mass has been celebrated.

Feast of the Seven Fishes

Every Italian dish has a story and some of the best stories center around Christmas food. Since this is the grandest of fasts, no cheese logs and crackers for us Italian Americans! On Christmas Eve we make the multi-course Feast of Seven Fishes, remembering Nonna Christina's belief that these fish represent the Seven Sacraments in the Church. Italians celebrate the last night of fasting for Advent without meat but with an astonishing array of carefully prepared fish dishes. Most Italian Americans serve salted cod (baccala), squid (calamari), eel, smelts and octopus for sure; shellfish can also be included to make up the seven. Younger generations have put lobster, tuna fish, oysters, clams, mussels and crab on the menu. Other Italians offer variations on the number of fishes served Christmas Eve; for instance, thirteen fishes represent Jesus and the twelve apostles.

Nonna Christina's ancestors were peasants and ate according to their class. The richer you were, the better food you could put on your Christmas Eve table. The best fish they could afford were the oily and salted varieties. Today, due to demand, the price has gone up significantly for Nonna's favorite fish. But with so many possibilities at hand, you can make your own combination of fishes to reach the desired number.

Many of our recipes are quite simple with few ingredients—austere for the fast but satisfyingly delicious for a feast. A good baccala can be the centerpiece of the meal.

Salt Cod (Baccala)

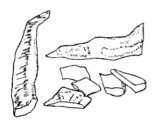

Any Italian nonna worth her sea salt will include baccala—salt cod—on her list of seven fishes. Imported from Scandinavia, baccala is preserved by salting and drying, so it must be soaked in water to remove the salt.

Nonna soaked it this way: Cover baccala with cold water and soak in the refrigerator for three days (signifying the Holy Trinity). Change the water three times a day, too. When the fish is soft and easy to cut, it is ready to use. Make sure pieces are pure white, with no yellow spots.

Nonna often steamed baccala in a tiny bit of water for 10 minutes, then drained it well before including it in a salad or casserole.

She liked to tell the children that all creatures of God are granted special blessings on Christmas Eve, citing animals' being able to speak at midnight as an example. One of her favorite tales was the "Miracle of Baccala," the legend of an old woman who had soaked many baccala. On Christmas Eve, one small fish returned to life and started swimming, so the old woman returned it to the sea.

Baked Salt Cod (Baked Baccala)
6 servings
Many of our baccala recipes are quite simple, with few ingredients—austere for the fast, but satisfyingly delicious for the feast. This dish was often the centerpiece of the meal.

- 2 pounds salt cod (baccala)
- 20 Italian black olives
- 1 onion, sliced
- 2 stalks celery, sliced
- 5 medium potatoes, peeled and cubed
- 2 tablespoons olive oil
- ⅛ teaspoon black pepper
- 1½ teaspoons parsley, chopped
- ½ teaspoon oregano

Heat oven to 350 degrees. In a baking dish, place salt cod, potatoes, onion and celery. Sprinkle olives over top, then add parsley and oregano. Drizzle top of casserole with olive oil. Bake, covered, for 30 to 40 minutes, until fish flakes. Remove cover during last 10 minutes of baking. For variety, add pitted green olives, crushed tomatoes, capers or raisins.

Salt Cod Salad (Baccala Salad)
6 servings

If you have home-canned peppers from a summer garden, creating this salad is the way to share them!

- 2 pounds steamed salt cod
- 1 ½ cups peppers, roasted
- 3 cloves garlic, chopped
- 20 cured black olives
- 1 ½ teaspoons parsley, chopped
- ½ teaspoon oregano
- ½ cup olive oil
- ¼ cup water
- 4 lemon wedges

In a large pot, steam the salt cod over boiling water for 10 minutes. Drain very well. Using a large serving platter, break salt cod into pieces and drizzle with olive oil, oregano, minced garlic and olives.

Garnish with parsley and oregano. Serve on a platter with fresh lemon wedges, and drizzle freshly squeezed lemon juice on top.

Baccala in Dough (Zeppole con Pesce)
6 servings

Our family serves these bite-sized pieces of dough as an appetizer or lunch on Christmas Eve. Munching on zeppoles while wrapping last-minute gifts is a fond childhood memory.

- 1 tablespoon dry yeast
- 1 ¼ cups warm water
- 3 cups flour
- 1 teaspoon salt
- 2 eggs, beaten
- ⅔ cup olive oil

Cut baccala into bite-sized pieces. Dissolve yeast in warm water. In a large bowl, add salt to flour. Make a well in flour and add remaining water, yeast, eggs and 2 tablespoons olive oil. Mix well. Let dough rise in a warm place until it is twice original size.

Heat remaining oil in fry pan. Break off chunks of dough and flatten in the palm of your hand. Place a piece of baccala in the middle of the dough, fold dough over and pinch shut. Fry until golden. I like to drain this crispy treat on a cookie rack before serving.

Octopus (Polpo)

Octopus has been celebrated by the Italians in art—and eating—since ancient times. It is sold in many sizes, but the smallest is the most tender. Octopus is usually available flash-frozen and already cleaned. If you buy it fresh, you'll need to clean it first by rinsing it under warm running water for one minute. At the center (hub) of the legs, you'll find the beak (a little, hard ball), the eyes and ink sac. Using a sharp knife, cut these away. Through the opening, turn octopus inside out and rinse well. Turn octopus right-side out again and cut into bite-sized pieces.

Octopus (Polpo) in Purgatory
6 servings

Nonna served this old recipe for octopus, claiming the Straits of Messina produced the sweetest polpo. But it doesn't matter where your octopus comes from—you'll be in heaven when you taste it!

2 pounds octopus, cleaned and cut into bite-sized pieces	½ cup water
2 pounds onions, sliced	1 garlic clove, minced
½ cup olive oil	½ teaspoon salt
1 cup white wine	½ cup white wine vinegar —optional

In a shallow pan, heat olive oil; add garlic, onions and salt. Sauté. Add the octopus and white wine. Stir for a few minutes, while the alcohol evaporates, then add water. Cover and simmer for 1½ hours or until tender. For a sharper taste, add the vinegar.

Anchovies

When I was a child, a big bite of strong, salty anchovies was overwhelming and the texture horrifying. I vowed never to eat them again, joining the ranks of Italians who "skeeve" anchovies. Still, my relatives loved them, and I found that anchovies are not a half-way taste: you either love them or you hate them.

Small, commonplace fish, anchovies were affordable to peasant families, and my ancestors learned to make the most of them. They are rich in healthy proteins and, because they have a shorter life cycle, anchovies accumulate fewer impurities from their environment. Nonna knew that when you sauté anchovies in olive oil, they literally melt away and meld into a rich, dramatic dish. The nutritional benefits from eating this fish give even the most ardent anchovy-hater reason to give them a second try.

Anchovies in Garlic Sauce
6 servings

1½ cups bread crumbs
1 pound spaghetti
⅓ cup olive oil

5 ounces anchovies (3 tins)
1 tablespoon black pepper

Toast bread crumbs in a pan over medium heat, stirring often until browned. Cook pasta.

Drain oil from 2 anchovy tins into another skillet. Chop the anchovy fillets and add the chopped fish to the second skillet along with olive oil. Cook until fish disappears in oil (2 to 3 minutes).

Drain pasta and toss it in serving bowl with anchovy oil mixture. Add freshly cracked pepper, then sprinkle ½ cup bread crumbs on top. From the third anchovy tin, arrange fish on top of the pasta. Serve with a bowl of the extra bread crumbs for topping.

Anchovy-Stuffed Christmas Peppers
6 servings

These anchovy-stuffed peppers have been a holiday hit for generations.

3 green peppers, seeded and cleaned	½ cup mozzarella cheese, shredded
3 red peppers, seeded and cleaned	¼ cup Parmesan cheese
3 tomatoes, peeled, seeded and diced	½ cup rice
3 cloves garlic, minced	½ teaspoon salt
1 onion, finely chopped	¼ teaspoon black pepper
3 tablespoons parsley, chopped	Additional Parmesan cheese
⅓ cup dry white wine	2 cups water
3 anchovy fillets, chopped	1 cup tomato sauce
4 tablespoons olive oil	

Preheat oven to 375 degrees. Using a sharp knife, cut off tops of peppers. Boil a large pot of water and blanch peppers for 4 minutes. Drain in colander.

Boil rice in 1 cup water until it is al dente (slightly undercooked). Rinse, drain and set aside.

In a large skillet, sauté onion in olive oil until translucent. Stir in anchovies and garlic, then mash them together. Add tomatoes and wine, cook for 3 minutes and remove from the heat. Add parsley, rice, mozzarella, salt, pepper and Parmesan cheese.

Dry insides of peppers, then spoon stuffing mix into each, filling to the top. Sprinkle with Parmesan cheese. Drizzle each pepper with olive oil. Place stuffed peppers in baking dish and add water ¼ of the way up the peppers. Bake for 25 to 30 minutes. Serve with a bowl of tomato sauce to ladle over the peppers.

Eel

Eel is well worth the extra effort it takes to prepare. Its sweet white flesh is considered a delicacy and an Italian Christmas Eve tradition. In fact, relatives pop in just to try a piece. Eel is loaded with vitamins and nutritious Omega-3 fatty acids. From ancient Roman times, Italian families have been paving the road to good health with every serving.

Going out of your way to buy good quality eel was always a must for the Italian-American family's Christmas Eve. Uncle Tony would make the trip to Newark to buy the fresh eel, found swimming in tubs in the fish markets. As children, we were enthralled watching the eel swim around the sink before my father would take it out back to skin it.

He'd set up a board and Uncle Tony would hold the eel in place. Father would make the sign of the cross, then nail the great serpent's head to the board. Sometimes Father needed to drop a large rock on its head to kill it, because no one had the heart to see the majestic eel struggle out of water. Then he would skin and clean it.

To Clean Live Eel

Drive a nail into the eel to hold it firmly to the cutting board or, more humanely, place the live eel in the freezer for 2 hours to kill it. Remove the eel and place it on a cutting board. Make a circular incision just below the eel's head. Using a towel or work gloves and a firm grip, forcefully peel back the skin and pull it all the way down the eel's body. Using a large, sharp knife, remove the head and discard it.

Before using, soak the eel in cold water for 30 minutes. Rinse it well under cold running water, rubbing off any residue with your fingers. Cut the eel into ½-inch pieces for use in recipes.

Fried Eel (Anguille Fritte)
6 servings

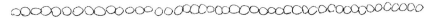

2 pounds cleaned eel	½ teaspoon salt
2 cups olive oil	¼ teaspoon pepper
2 cups flour	

Cut eel into 1-inch pieces for frying. Dredge each piece of eel in flour, making sure to coat all sides.

Fill a deep skillet or heavy pot with cooking oil to 2-inch depth and heat over medium heat. Make sure oil is hot enough before you begin by throwing a pinch of flour into the hot oil. If bubbles come up from the flour, oil is ready.

Fry eel until brown on both sides. Take out and drain for 5 minutes on a cookie rack. Sprinkle eel with salt and pepper. Transfer to serving platter. Serve with lemon wedges.

Baked Eel
6 servings

2 pounds cleaned eel	1 teaspoon oregano
½ cup bread crumbs	1 tablespoon parsley, chopped
3 tablespoons Romano cheese	4 tablespoons olive oil
2 cloves garlic, chopped	

Place the eel in a baking dish and season fish with salt and pepper. Mix the next 5 ingredients and sprinkle over eel. Drizzle top of fish with olive oil.

Before baking add ½ inch of water in dish. Bake uncovered at 375 degrees for 45 minutes. Eel should be a nice golden brown.

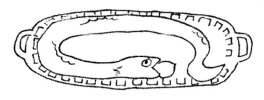

Squid (Calamari)

Why say "squid" when you can be Italian and say "calamari"? That's so much more romantic! Calamari is deliciously tender in tomato sauce, served over steaming linguine.

Squid in Fresh Tomato Sauce (Calamari al Sugo)
6 servings

- 2 pounds squid, cut into ¼-inch rings
- 1 large onion, chopped
- 2 cloves garlic, minced
- 2 cups crushed tomatoes
- 1 tablespoon parsley, chopped
- 1 teaspoon basil
- 1 teaspoon oregano
- ½ teaspoon salt
- ⅛ teaspoon pepper
- ¼ cup olive oil
- ¼ cup red wine

To clean the squid, separate the mantle from the body containing head and legs. Grasp the mantle in one hand and pull off the head and leg section with the other hand. Pull and gently twist off head, eyes and legs; discard them. Clean out the insides of the mantle with your fingertips, rubbing away any loose tissue while running cold water over squid.

Turn mantle inside-out and thoroughly clean again with fingertips, rubbing away any loose tissue while running cold water over squid. Keeping mantle inside-out, repeat cleaning thoroughly with fingertips and cold running water.

With a very sharp knife, slice squid mantle into ¼-inch rings, pressing firmly on knife to cut all the way through mantle.

Heat olive oil in a heavy skillet over medium heat. Sauté squid rings in oil and garlic for 1 minute before adding onions, parley, basil and oregano. Stir in salt and pepper, then cook mixture for 5 minutes.

Add wine, cover and simmer for 5 minutes more. Add tomatoes and simmer for 30 minutes until squid is tender. Place squid in a large bowl atop linguine cooked al dente. Serve at once.

Fried Squid (Calamari)
6 servings

Nonna wouldn't even use a knife to prepare the squid for this recipe. She'd just use her fingers to tear and rub away unusable sections. Remember to allow ½ pound of uncleaned squid per serving.

3 pounds squid	3 tablespoons olive oil
1 cup flour	

Separate the legs and tentacles; they can be fried intact. Cut squid mantle into ¼-inch rings. Coat in flour and fry in olive oil until golden. Drain and serve with a bowl of tomato sauce on the side, if you like, for dipping. Don't bother with forks. My children can't wait to eat these yummy, delicate rings with their fingers!

Cuttlefish (Seppia)

Our uncles would argue over the proper cleaning of this Italian favorite. The cuttlefish or "seppia" in Italian, is similar to octopus and contains a sac filled with a liquidy brown ink.

When cleaning the fish, they'd warn, the sac must not be punctured or it could mean certain death! Every Christmas Eve the same animated conversation would build among the men at the table.

"Who cleaned the seppia?" Because God forbid, somebody might be poisoned at the table while eating it. You could be taking your life into your own hands by eating seppia!

This made Christmas Eve dinner very mysterious and exciting, even though today we know it is just a legend. Our grandmothers really did know best—seppia is perfectly safe to eat and is now in vogue with home cooks.

Great chefs have used the ink sac as an ingredient to color and flavor the risotto! And great writers and photographers have used the ink for writing and creating a genre of photography like no other.

Be brave—they are easy to clean!

Cuttlefish Risotto (Seppia Risotto)
6 servings

Making homemade risotto is really a lesson in love. It needs attention. You can't just put a lid on it and walk away. But its seductive creaminess and intense flavor are worth it.

- 2 pounds cuttlefish
- 2 small onions
- ¼ cup olive oil
- 1 cup dry white wine
- 1 clove garlic
- 1 teaspoon chopped parsley
- 10 ounces arborio rice
- 1 quart vegetable stock
- 2 tablespoons butter
- ⅛ teaspoon salt
- ⅛ teaspoon pepper

The top half of the cuttlefish is known as the helmet. Holding the cuttlefish under running water, pull the helmet away from the tentacles. Gently peel off the thin membrane of skin covering the helmet. Stick your finger inside the helmet and gently pull out the innards. The ink sac—it's oval and about as big as a nickel—will come out along with everything else. Because a little ink goes a long way, double- or triple-bag the ink sac for later use. The mouth and beak are found between the tentacles. Pull beak out and cut away the eyes. Rinse tentacles thoroughly.

Cut the cuttlefish into thin strips. Using a large skillet, brown one of the onions and garlic in oil. Remove garlic when browned and add the cuttlefish, parsley and wine. Continue cooking the cuttlefish approximately 15 minutes or until cooked through.

In another large skillet, cook the second onion in 2 tablespoons of melted butter until just soft, but not brown. Add the ink sac and stir. Add a small ladleful of broth and turn the heat to low. Keep stirring the rice as it soaks up the liquid. Pour in small amounts of broth and continuously stir until the rice has been cooking for 15 to 18 minutes. Rice should be al dente or firm to the bite. The risotto should be creamy but not soupy.

Let the risotto stand for a minute or 2 before scooping it into serving bowls. Top each bowl with a ladleful of cuttlefish. Sprinkle with salt and pepper if desired. No cheese is needed for this dish.

Smelts

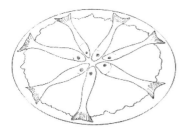

Smelts are a tiny, dainty fish. Nonna served them with the heads still on because the entire fish can be eaten. Throughout the year she would serve fried smelts on a bed of Swiss chard seasoned with garlic. But for the Feast of Seven Fishes, Nonna liked to use this dish to symbolize the Christmas Star, replacing the chard with broccoli rabe as a winter vegetable.

Don't stint on the greens' cooking time, because you'll want to twirl some around your fork with each bite of fish. For dramatic effect, Nonna artfully arranged the smelts like the spokes of a wheel, with tails pointing outward.

Smelts in a Christmas Star with Chard
6 servings

4 dozen smelts, cleaned
1 cup flour
Large bunches of broccoli rabe, Swiss chard or spinach
1 teaspoon salt
1 teaspoon pepper
2 lemons, sliced thin
½ cup olive oil

Wash and dry smelts, then roll each in flour. Using a large skillet, heat olive oil and cook smelts until browned on each side. Drain them on a cake rack.

While the smelts brown, cook greens in salted water until tender. Spoon greens onto a large round serving platter. Arrange smelts like the spokes of a wheel on top of greens. You can serve this dish with cocktail forks and plates as an appetizer.

Seafood Stew (Cioppino)
12 servings

Don't let the French awe you with their Bouillabaisse—the Italians have their own version of fish stew called Cioppino. Both dishes got their humble beginnings from the fish unsold at the end of the day. Just think of Bouillabaisse as the snooty French relative to Cioppino. The Italians decided to add a tomato-based broth and omit the saffron. Keep everybody as happy as clams, try this version which is Italian with a nod to our French cousins.

- 2½ pounds tomatoes, peeled and crushed
- 1 onion, chopped
- 7 cloves of garlic
- 1 cup tomato sauce
- 1 teaspoon basil, chopped
- 1 teaspoon oregano, chopped
- 1 teaspoon thyme
- 1 tablespoon salt
- ¼ teaspoon black pepper
- ¼ teaspoon cayenne pepper
- ¼ cup parsley, chopped
- 12 slices Italian bread, toasted
- ⅓ cup olive oil
- 1 cup dry white wine
- ½ cup water
- 1 pound shrimp
- 1 pound bay scallops
- 1 dozen mussels
- 18 cherrystone clams
- 2 pounds rock lobster tails
- ½ pound crabmeat
- 1 pound cod fillets

The best way to prepare this stew is to prep the vegetables and seafood ahead of time. Thoroughly clean the clams and mussels, dry the scallops, remove lobster from shells, peel and de-vein shrimp, cut up crabmeat into ½-inch sections, rinse cod in cold water and cut into 1-inch pieces.

In a heavy 8-quart pot, sauté onion and garlic until translucent. Add wine and cook for 2 minutes. Add crushed tomatoes, tomato sauce and water, then stir. Season with basil, oregano, thyme, salt and pepper. Stir to blend, turn heat to medium high and cook until just boiling. Cover and simmer for ½ hour, stirring occasionally.

Seafood Stew (Cioppino) continued

Slice a loaf of Italian bread for toasting. About 30 minutes before stew is to be served, preheat oven to 350 degrees. Place sliced bread on baking sheet and toast in oven until browned.

Add lobster and crab to stockpot. Cover and simmer 4 minutes. Add cod and cover. Discard any clams or mussels that do not close when tapped, then add both to stockpot, cover and simmer for 10 minutes. Lower heat to medium low and add scallops. Cover and cook 5 minutes or until scallops are tender and all clams and mussels have opened.

Serve the cioppino in a large soup tureen. Ladle into soup bowls atop a slice of toasted Italian bread.

Tip: Busy cooks can make the broth a day ahead, then reheat it and follow the steps for adding the seafood. On Christmas Eve, my family enjoys Cioppino served over plates of angel hair pasta. The seafood makes a wonderful presentation, and pasta stretches this stew to feed a large crowd.

Don't forget to have lots of bread to sop up the goodness!

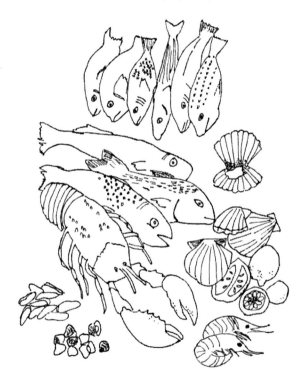

Antipasto & Vegetables

My aunts liked to wear Christmas aprons over their church clothes on Christmas Eve. The women would cook and the men would sit. My uncles would sit in the living room and sip homemade wine while the women, so rarely together all at once, taught secrets of the Italian rituals to other female family members.

The preparations began early on Christmas Eve day. I remember being in a crowded kitchen preparing the fish dishes with my mother and aunts. People would be bumping into each other in the tight space. When someone needed to use a big bread knife, she'd yell out, "Nobody move—I have a knife."

The antipasto dish is served before the traditional Italian pasta meal or main course, but it is not essential to Italian dining. Nonna served an antipasto course only for special occasions or holidays. Similar to an appetizer, the antipasto whets the appetite and heightens anticipation of the meal to come; however, it never satisfies hunger.

For the antipasto, Nonna, a creative cook and gardener, took advantage of many different kinds of foods that would not be substantial enough to be served as a main course. The family garden—the ultimate labor of love—provided a pantry cupboard stocked with rows of colorful glass jars. These vegetables, picked at the height of the season and preserved in oil for use throughout the year, supplied many of the ingredients for her antipasto.

So we could count on such favorites as marinated artichokes, roasted peppers and marinated mushrooms, along with a colorful array of olives and handmade mozzarella balls.

Now as then, guests and family can enjoy cocktails and antipasto while the finishing touches are put on the main course in the kitchen.

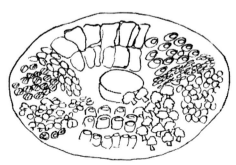

Olives, Super Food

Like an Italian son, the olive was cherished and could do no wrong. Olives in colorful assortments were added to Nonna Christina's antipasto and can be attractively served up stuffed with cheeses, such as Gorgonzola or blue cheese and plunked into Italian vodka for martinis or cocktails. Nonna believed that offering olives to her guests upon arrival was blessing them with a long and peaceful life. That turns out to be true since olives contain mono-saturated fats that can help lower cholesterol levels and reduce the risk of heart attacks.

My family still holds the olive in high esteem because of its deep connection to the church and the Bible stories. Nonna believed olives have sacred healing attributes for body and spirit. Monks in ancient times planted many olive trees and cultivated them on terraces overlooking the sea. For centuries, olive oil has been used in church rituals to anoint the body, beginning at birth and all through to the end of life.

A Hebrew tradition tells how Adam, anticipating the moment of his death, asked an angel to place three seeds on his tongue. One of the trees that sprouted was the olive tree. In the Garden of Gethsemane, where Jesus prayed before his crucifixion, lives an olive tree reported to be 3,000 years old. In Grosseto, Italy, there is an olive tree believed to be 3,500 years old; it is called l'ulivo della strega—the witch's olive tree.

The magical fruit appears in colors ranging from purples and reds to browns and greens. Green olives are picked before they are ripe; black olives have been allowed to ripen to maturity on the tree. Most olives are cured for between 2 weeks and several months before being eaten. Curing agents—lye, brine or salt—determine the flavor and texture.

Nonna would never use canned olives—if she didn't have home-grown olives, she would find a market that cured olives on the premises. A staple of Mediterranean cuisine, olives come in at least 35 species. The most popular Italian varieties are Castelvetrano (Sicily), green Cerignola (Apulia), Taggiasca (Liguria) and Gaeta.

Marinated Mushrooms

Generations of Italians have used mushrooms as the foundation for some of the most famous dishes. Back in Italy, Nonna never revealed where she'd find the mushrooms, seeking them after a rain and always leaving some behind so the spores would multiply into another harvest for her to gather the next time.

Mushrooms make an outstanding addition to your antipasto platter. Ideally, mushrooms shouldn't be washed, but cleaned with a soft brush or sharp knife to remove all traces of soil. Choose mushrooms that are fresh and firm.

1¼ pounds mushrooms, cleaned and sliced very thin
¼ cup olive oil
2 lemons, squeezed
3 cloves garlic, minced fine
Salt and pepper
Paper-thin shavings of Parmigiano-Reggiano

Rely on your taste buds when putting this marinade together, changing the proportion of ingredients as you wish. Leave mushrooms to marinate in the refrigerator for about three hours before serving. Top with the cheese.

Fresh Marinated Artichokes

Here's a bit of Italian advice on how to deal with personal problems: Handle them the way you would handle an artichoke, which is "one leaf at a time, then set the choke free." Making your own marinated artichokes is so easy you'll soon be giving jars away as stocking stuffers!.

2 dozen small artichokes
1 cup wine vinegar
4 tablespoons parsley, chopped
1 cup virgin olive oil
4 cloves of garlic

Steam artichokes until a leaf pulls out easily. Don't overcook them. Remove leaves and store them in the refrigerator in a nice aioli to use another day. Remove chokes and trim.

Mix vinegar, oil, garlic, parsley and artichoke hearts. Stir, cover tightly and refrigerate for at least a day before serving. Keep in the refrigerator where the artichokes will gain flavor for up to 3 weeks.

Broccoli al Dente in Oil and Garlic
6 servings

2 pounds fresh broccoli
3 cloves garlic, minced
6 tablespoons olive oil

Wash broccoli and peel stems. Boil in about an inch of water in a large pot, using steamer if possible. Cook for 8 minutes or until stems are tender when pierced. Remove from the heat and drain.

Using a large skillet, heat olive oil and garlic but do not let garlic brown. Add broccoli and cook it for 4 minutes, turning it to coat it in olive oil. Season the dish with salt and pepper and serve.

Green Beans and Fresh Tomatoes (Fabiolini Verdi con Pomodori)
6 servings

12 ounces fresh plum tomatoes
1 pound fresh string beans
1 onion
4 tablespoons olive oil
½ cup white wine
Basil

Snap ends off beans, wash and drain. In a large skillet heat olive oil, add onion and sauté until soft. Add diced tomatoes and cook over medium heat until they become soft (about 8 minutes). Add the wine, basil and the beans, turning them over to coat them completely in the liquid.

Cover and cook over medium heat for 20 minutes. Stir and season with salt and pepper. You can add a little more wine or water to bring the liquid level back from evaporating.

Roasted Fennel (Finocchio)

Finocchio is a root vegetable that dates back to ancient Rome and has long been praised for its medicinal purposes, especially for aiding digestion. It resembles an onion bulb, but has an anise-inspired sweetness that is wonderful with fish. It helps to munch on some if you are feeling too full after a meal or experience "agita"—Italian-speak for heartburn.

The entire finocchio plant can be eaten. Fronds are perfect for decorating the tops of salads. It's delicious served raw (pinzimonio) or roasted in the oven with a little olive oil.

Three or 4 bulbs of cooked finocchio are equivalent in volume to 3 or 4 potatoes. For something a little fancier, try boiled finocchio topped with melted Fontina cheese.

Finocchio with Parmesan
6 servings

4 fennel bulbs
Butter for braising
Salt and pepper
½ cup Parmesan cheese, freshly grated

Trim and wash the fennel, then cut bulbs into equal-sized chunks. Boil for 5 minutes in salted water. Drain very well.

Warm butter to fill bottom of a large skillet and add fennel. Sauté, stirring gently over medium heat until fennel is tender. Sprinkle lightly with salt, pepper and Parmesan. Serve hot.

Finocchio with Fontina
6 servings

3 to 4 bulbs fennel
Fennel seeds
Salt
¼ pound Fontina cheese, shredded

Boil the fennel and a few fennel seeds in salted water until fork-tender. Drain and cut into cubes, then stir in the cheese. Spread washed, dried and minced fennel fronds on top of the vegetable. Cover the dish with a lid so that the cheese melts completely. Serve as a side dish for fish.

Roasted Peppers
6 servings

Two dozen fresh peppers (use both sweet and hot)
Olive oil

Slice peppers in half, removing most of the seeds but not all. Coat the bottom of a baking dish with olive oil. Brush generous amounts of olive oil (don't use extra-virgin for this) over peppers and in between crevices. Roast in slow heat at 350 degrees for 3 hours. Place in container to chill in refrigerator. These peppers will last 2 weeks in the refrigerator.

Blood Orange Salad
6 servings

This salad has a traditional place on the Italian Christmas Eve table. It is made with two kinds of oranges: navel oranges and blood oranges, so-called for their vibrant, juicy-red insides, popular in Europe as Tarocco, Moro and Sanguinello oranges. You can find them here in the grocery store as either blood oranges or by their Italian names. Select in their prime.

6 oranges, peeled and sliced ¼-inch thick with seeds removed
¼ cup orange juice
½ teaspoon salt
¼ to ½ teaspoon black pepper
1 pound Kalamata olives
3 tablespoons extra-virgin olive oil

Fan orange slices on a large oval or round platter, alternating slices of blood orange with slices of navel orange. Sprinkle with salt and freshly cracked black peppercorn. Drizzle platter with orange juice—just a spritzing, so be careful. Oranges should just appear juicy from the orange juice. Spread olives out around platter. Drizzle 2 to 3 tablespoons of extra-virgin olive oil over the entire platter. Taste for seasoning.

Midnight Mass

Like the first relatives to arrive at the hospital after the birth of a newborn, Italian Catholics choose to attend midnight mass since it is the first chance to receive Holy Communion and for the priest to celebrate mass on this important holiday.

Often generations of families go to mass together. During Advent, the Catholic Church displays only the Advent Wreath. At midnight mass, all of the candles are lit to signify Advent has come to a climax. A crèche or nativity scene is set out, and the statue of Baby Jesus is lovingly placed in the manger. The altar comes alive with festive greenery and candles. The choirs sing out in angelic voices. Red, white and green, the colors of Italy, are also used to symbolize Christmas. The green symbolizes Hope. Red reminds us of Jesus' martyrdom, and white and gold stand for purity and royalty. The King of Kings is born. Italian Catholics welcome the Christ Child, the Baby Jesus.

For God so loved the world that He gave his only Son;
that whoever believes in Him should not perish but have eternal life.
–John 3:16

Cookie Exchange

After going to midnight mass someone might start cooking all over again. The long fast is over—we can eat meat again. Ham or sausage with peppers might be prepared as family and friends come in from church. Someone will plug in the Christmas crèche display. The Advent Wreath will be lit with the last purple candle because Christ has been born! It's time for merriment with drinks and a toast with the Dessertina of nuts, fruit and Italian cookies.

I'd like to think that Italian women established the "Cookie Exchange"! In our homes trays and trays of Italian cookies are lined up on the sofas in the weeks prior to Christmas Eve. We take the baking of our recipes very seriously. Most of us have a cookie we are famous for, and the recipe is a guarded secret. My mother and her sisters practically made the cookie exchange a ceremony! It was a ritual: each relative would travel far and wide to trade and build cookie trays. I remember the 5 sisters baking a huge assortment of Christmas cookies and then converging in one house to exchange them. Everybody would be talking at once and cookies, cookies, everywhere! It took hours to settle, with each woman bringing home a vast assortment of delicious cookies. Then on Christmas Eve huge silver trays of homemade Italian cookies are placed on the table after mass.

Chocolate Pepper Cookie

This is a traditional Italian recipe handed down through my family. It makes a large batch, perfect for a cookie exchange.

3 cups flour	1 teaspoon nutmeg
½ cup sugar	½ teaspoon salt
½ cup cocoa	2 eggs
2½ teaspoons baking powder	½ cup solid shortening
1 teaspoon cinnamon	1 tablespoon jam or jelly
1 teaspoon ground cloves	(makes the cookie moist)
1 teaspoon black pepper	½ cup milk

Mix all ingredients, adding the milk last in small amounts. The dough should be dry and heavy. Roll out small balls the size of a walnut. Bake on greased cookie sheet for 10 minutes at 375 degrees.

Glaze: Use equal parts powdered sugar and milk; stir well.

Wait for cookies to cool and place them in a large bowl. Slowly pour glaze on top and toss them gently with your hands. Line up on waxed paper until glaze sets.

Almond Cookies

1 egg	2 teaspoons Amaretto
½ cup soft butter	¾ cup almonds
1¼ cups flour	½ cup sugar

Cream butter and sugar. Beat in eggs, Amaretto and almonds. Slowly add the flour. Drop by tablespoonfuls onto ungreased baking sheet. Bake at 400 degrees until they are brown at the edges.

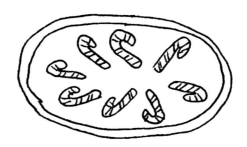

Candy Cane Cookies

My childhood favorite, this recipe for edible ornaments turns worktime festive when children are asked to help prepare—it's a twist!

¾ cup butter, softened	½ teaspoon vanilla extract
1 cup sugar	2½ cups all-purpose flour
1 large egg	Red food coloring

Cream butter and sugar. Add egg and beat well. Stir in vanilla, then gradually mix in flour.

Divide the dough in half. Color one half with red food coloring and leave the other half plain.

Roll out a tablespoon of red dough and a tablespoon of plain until they reach about 6 inches long. Twist them into a candy cane, pinching the ends. Make same with rest of dough.

Bake on ungreased cookie sheet for 8 to 10 minutes or until set, but not brown. Makes about 25 cookies.

"S" Cookies

3 cups flour
3½ teaspoons baking powder
1 cup sugar
1 stick butter
1 teaspoon vanilla extract
4 eggs
½ cup milk

Roll out and shape dough into little 'S' shaped cookies the size of your thumb. Bake on greased cookie sheet at 375 degrees for 10 minutes.

Option: Try adding chocolate chips to this batter before shaping.

Sister Assunta's Little White Wafer Cookies

Sister Assunta didn't own an electric mixer but no matter, because electric beaters would make this mixture too light. Sister would use a fork and beat these by hand for about one hour, until yolks and sugar transformed into a creamy white mixture.

6 egg yolks
¾ cup granulated sugar

Preheat oven to 250 degrees.

Use pleated cupcake liners to hold batter for each cookie. Fill ¼ of liner. Line up on cookie sheet and place in oven. Turn off the heat. Leave cookies in the oven until they have risen but centers are still creamy (about 1 hour).
If oven loses heat too soon, you can turn on the heat again to 180 degrees.

Remove cookies and place them on wire rack to cool completely; arrange on a serving platter.

White Italian Snowballs

2½ cups flour
½ cup sugar
3½ teaspoons baking powder (heaping)

3 eggs
½ cup milk
½ teaspoon vanilla extract
½ cup shortening

(glaze: 1 cup powdered sugar, 1 cup milk)

Mix ingredients and roll into walnut-sized balls, Bake on greased cookie sheet for 10 to 15 minutes, or until edges are brown.

Mix equal amounts of powdered sugar and milk in a bowl. Blend well. Dip each cookie in icing. Nonna often added a few drops of anisette flavor to the icing. You can leave icing white or tint with food coloring in Advent colors, making cookies pink and/or lavender.

White Italian Drop Cookies

White icing on these cookies represents the purity of the newborn Baby Jesus.

3 eggs
½ cup sugar
3 teaspoons baking powder

½ teaspoon vanilla extract
1¼ sticks butter
2 cups flour

Mix eggs, sugar, butter and vanilla. Mix baking powder in with flour. Add flour to wet mixture. Dough has to be soft. Drop with teaspoon onto greased pans and bake at 350 degrees for 10 to 12 minutes.

For icing, blend equal parts powdered sugar and milk.

Anisette Cookies

    5 to 6 cups flour   1 cup sugar
    4 teaspoons baking powder   2 teaspoons anise extract
    6 eggs   Pinch of salt
    1 cup shortening

Mix flour, baking powder and sugar together in a bowl. Add shortening, cream together and mix. In a separate bowl, beat eggs and anise extract, add to the flour mixture and mix more into dough. Roll into balls. Bake at 350 degrees for 10 to 12 minutes.

Glaze for Anisette Cookies:

    1 pound powdered sugar   3 drops anise extract
    ¼ cup cold milk

Start off by adding 1 tablespoon at a time of cold milk to the powdered sugar; the density of the sugar decreases as the cold milk is added. Mix and combine until desired consistency, add drops of anise extract. Coat frosting on top and sides of cookie.

Strufoli

Nonna Pitarra made fried dough balls, dipped in honey, nuts and candy every year to mark the Advent season for her eleven children. She remembered her neighbors, especially the neighbor who kept the honey bees. Nothing says "you're remembered" quite like a heaping plate of warm Strufoli.

3 cups flour
4 eggs
¼ cup butter
½ cup sugar
½ teaspoon salt
2 teaspoons baking powder

½ tablespoon orange zest
1 ½ cups honey (from local bees!)
¾ cup pine nuts
2 ¼ ounces confetti candy or sprinkles
oil for frying

Mix the first 7 ingredients into a dough. Roll dough into rope as thick as a pencil. Cut into 1-inch pieces. Roll these pieces into little balls the size of a quarter.

In a deep pot, place oil 2 inches deep, heat and fry dough balls until golden. Drain on paper towels.

Use a saucepan and boil honey gently over medium heat for 3 minutes. Add dough balls, stir with wooden spoon to gently coat. Remove Strufoli with a slotted spoon onto a large serving platter.

Sprinkle with nuts and candy, best served or given away warm!

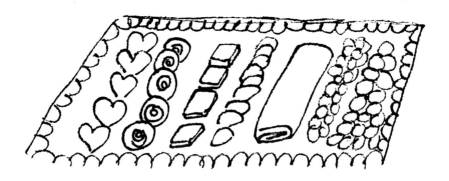

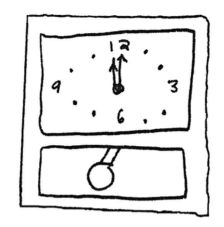

Tiramisu

This recipe means "pick me up" in Italian, and eating this fluffy layered concoction will do just that for your spirit!

1½ pounds Mascarpone cheese
5 eggs at room temperature, separated
½ cup sugar
Ladyfingers or sliced sponge cake, cut to fit bottom of baking dish snugly with no spaces in between

½ cup strong espresso
4 tablespoons brandy or rum – optional
Unsweetened cocoa powder to sprinkle on top

In a bowl, beat cheese until soft.

In a second bowl, beat egg yolks and sugar (all but 1 tablespoon) until fluffy and yellow. Slowly beat in Mascarpone. In another bowl, using a wire whisk, beat egg whites and salt into stiff peaks. Fold eggs into cheese mixture. Prepare espresso.

Line deep baking dish with lady fingers or sponge cake cut to fit dish bottom tightly. Sprinkle the espresso over cake until moist but not soaked. Cover with half the egg and cheese mixture.

Add another layer of cake, moistening with coffee and the rest of the egg mixture. Sprinkle cocoa powder on top, use liberally.

Refrigerate 2 hours before serving.

Chestnuts

Our Italian ancestors were hard-working, common people who appreciated the great value of the small chestnut. Peasants tended chestnut trees and prepared the nuts with love for their families. Part of their humble everyday meals, the chestnut was a staple food, used for sustenance. Chestnuts are different from other nuts because they are low in calories and low in fat. Similar in nutrition to brown rice, they were often ground into flour to extend bread products and replace cereals. Chestnuts contain vitamin C and are a great source of trace minerals.

Uncle Jimmy was in the wholesale fruit business, and on Christmas Eve he provided a towering basket filled with colorful tangerines, oranges, dried fruit and nuts. Nutcrackers were brought out to crack hazelnuts, acorns and walnuts at the table. Chestnuts were roasted. Sometimes, even the priest would stop by on the pretense he was only coming for coffee, but then stay and eat because after the long mass, he was hungry too.

Italian-Americans today are still enjoying this versatile super food. Every time I cut crosses into chestnut tops before roasting, it brings to mind the importance of the season.

Drunken Chestnuts (Castagne Ubriache)

Select chestnuts that are plump and fresh. Cut small crosses in the top of the shells and roast for 30 minutes. Peel off the shell and serve. Chestnuts are also flavorful topped with melted garlic butter.

2½ pounds fresh chestnuts
1 cup dry red wine
¼ cup sugar

Roast chestnuts, peel and skin. Cook wine and sugar on top of the stove. When sugar dissolves, add the chestnuts. Cook and stir until wine is reduced to a thick syrup, about 30 minutes. Serve warm in bowls.

Chestnut Pudding (Bodino de Castagne)

1 pound chestnuts
18 ounces milk
2 to 3 drops vanilla extract
4 ounces almonds
2 ounces sugar
Pinch of salt
½ cup half and half

Boil chestnuts 30 minutes, peel and skin. In a large pot, add milk, vanilla, pinch of salt; stir and add chestnuts. Cook for 35 minutes, covered, over medium heat until chestnuts are very soft. Press chestnuts and their cooking liquid through a metal strainer into another saucepan. Toast almonds and chop. Gently heat chestnut puree, add sugar and half of the almonds. Remove from heat. Stir in half and half. Mix into a mold or deep dish. Chill 3 hours. To serve, invert pudding and turn onto serving plate. Sprinkle top with remaining almonds.

Beverages

For the home bartender, you can easily turn a tabletop into a bar area and all you need are a few essentials: a spoon, ice, ice bucket, a Boston shaker (stainless steel cup with tight fitting lid), a shot glass, Rocks and martini glasses, or other 8-ounce glasses of your choice.

Any beverage can be used for the ultimate Italian toast of "Stata Buon" by repeating these words and touching your glass to another's. In Italian these words translate into "Stay Well," which is a favorite toast among our family.

Campari—Italian Sunset (Cordial)

>   2 ounces of Campari
>   6 ounces orange juice

Fill an 8-ounce glass with ice. Pour in 6 ounces of orange juice. For dramatic effect, pour Campari into glass following the orange juice by "floating method." Float Campari into glass by inverting a spoon over glass and streaming Campari gently, allowing it to run off the back of spoon into orange juice. Enjoy Italian Sunset!

Rocco's Italian Kiss

  1 ounce Amaretto
  1 ounce Triple Sec
  1 ounce vodka
  ½ ounce rum
  ½ ounce cranberry juice
  ½ ounce orange juice
  Splash of Grenadine

Mix all ingredients with ice. Shake well and strain into a martini glass. Garnish with an orange slice.

The Maniscalco Mind Eraser (fagetaboutit)

  2 ounces Chambord
  2 ounces vodka
  2 ounces Sprite

Serve this drink over ice. Using a spoon, pour liquors into a glass in layers. Drink the Mind Eraser through a straw, all at once.

Golden Cadillac

Rocco is as proud of this drink as his father was of his car.

  1 ½ ounces white cream de cacao
  ¾ ounce Galliano
  1 ounce light cream

Mix well. Strain into a martini glass.

Italian Hot Chocolate
4 servings

    2 cups milk
    2 cups heavy cream
    2 vanilla beans, broken up in your hand
    8 ounces bittersweet chocolate
    2 tablespoons cocoa

Stir milk and heavy cream together in a medium saucepan. Add the broken vanilla bean. Heat the liquid to boiling. Stir in the chocolate and cocoa, stirring continuously until the chocolate is melted, then reduce the heat to low. Cook the mixture for 3 minutes. Take out the vanilla beans. Serve the hot chocolate with whipped cream.

Italian Christmas Eve Punch

    2 ounces orange juice
    2 ounces pineapple juice
    2 ounces cranberry juice

Mix all the juices and add a splash of Sprite or ginger ale. Serve over ice.

Homemade Anisette Liqueur

    3 cups vodka
    1 cup sugar
    3 tablespoons anise seeds
    ½ cup water

Use a clean glass container with a tight lid. Combine vodka and anise seeds, then store at room temperature for 1 to 2 weeks. Shake occasionally. Taste and strain.

Mix sugar and water in a pot, bring to a boil, let boil for 3 minutes. Skim top if needed. Mix the anise vodka and simple syrup. Pour into a glass bottle through a coffee filter-lined funnel. Age 1 month before serving. Traditionally served on Christmas Eve, it makes a great stocking stuffer too.

In many households, after a heavy meal, it is a custom to serve anisette or sambuca, both of which are believed to aid in digestion. Toasting with sambuca is led by the family patriarch, but the ladies join in too, sometimes serving sambuca as "Ammazzacaffe" (coffee killer) after the coffee. Our families enjoy it as an alternative to sugar in coffee. Although sambuca is typically transparent, when Rocco serves sambuca my favorite way, "on the rocks," the ice turns sambuca a thick white color.

Sambuca Toast:

1 ounce sambuca served in shot glass
3 coffee beans or espresso beans dropped on top
Matches for lighting on fire!

Start with shot glasses filled with sambuca. Drop in 3 coffee beans. With a match, light the sambuca on fire in the shot glass. Carefully touch glasses while repeating aloud, "To health, happiness and prosperity!" Everyone downs their shot at once. For maximum effect and safety, drink shot within 3 to 4 seconds after lighting, as the fire could cause the rim of the glass to get hot. It is recommended that you chew on the coffee beans after the toast because they release a robust flavor that intermingles with the taste of the sambuca.

Where to Shop

Balducci's
15 Palmer Ave.
Scarsdale, NY | 914-722-0200

Brooklyn Fare
200 Sohermerhorn St.
Brooklyn, NY | 718-243-0050

Calandra's Italian Bakery
204 First Ave.
Newark, NJ | 973-484-5598

Calandra's Cheese
350 East Lawn Road
Nazareth, PA | 610-759-2299

Caldwell Seafood
390 Bloomfield Ave.
Caldwell, NJ | 973-226-2031

Citarella's
2135 Broadway (Westside) NY
1313 3rd Ave. (Eastside) NY
424 N. 6th Ave. (Village) NY

**Danny 'D' & Denise's
 No Reservations Deli**
7540 Windsor Drive, Suite 112
Allentown, PA | 610-841-3637

Gerrity's
801 Wyoming Ave.
West Pittston, PA | 570-654-3444

Giant Food Stores
3070 W. Tilghman St.
Allentown, PA | 610-351-2091

Go Fish Seafood
Reading, PA
619 Penn Ave. | 610-376-6446
2934 N. 5th Street Hwy. | 610-921-8862

Heckenbergers Seafood
Allentown Fairgrounds Farmers Market
1835 Chew St.
Allentown, PA | 610-770-0860

Ippolito's Seafood
1300 Dickinson St.
Philadelphia, PA | 215-389-8906

Kings
650 Valley Rd.
Upper Montclair, NJ | 973-509-4828

La Dolce Vita Italian Bakery
5531 Hamilton Blvd.
Wescosville, PA | 610-395-8875

La Dolce Pastry Shop
655 Rossville Ave.
Staten Island, NY | 718-356-9864

Little Italy Food Center
1402 S. Main St.
Phillipsburg, NJ | 908-213-1800

Pastificio
1528 Packer Ave.
Philadelphia, PA | 215-467-1111

Palmer's Seafood
900 Jefferson Place
Rochester, NY | 585-272-9470

Plaza Pastry Shop
39 Franklin Ave.
Nutley, NJ | 973-661-0092

Rome Sweet Rome
54 Main St.
Plymouth, MA | 508-732-0012

Samuels & Son Seafood Co.
3400 S. Lawrence St.
Philadelphia, Pa | 215-336-7810

Sea Breeze Fish Market – Manhattan
541 Ninth Ave.
New York, NY 10018 | 212-563-7537

Sea Breeze Fish – Amboy Road
Located Inside Top Tomato
4045 Amboy Rd.
Staten Island, NY | 718-605-3257

Sea Breeze Fish – Bay Street
Located Inside Top Tomato
1071 Bay St.
Staten Island, NY | 718-981-8571

Sea Breeze Fish – Page Avenue
Located Inside Top Tomato
240 Page Ave.
Staten Island, NY | 718-984-0477

Sea Breeze Fish – Victory Blvd.
Located Inside Met Food
1795 Victory Blvd.
Staten Island, NY | 718-524-0833

Sea Breeze Fish – Bronx
Located Inside Big Deal Super Market
1018B Morris Park Ave.
Bronx, NY | 718-824-7571

Sea Breeze Fish – New Jersey
Located Inside Livoti's Old World Market
1077P State Highway 34
Aberdeen, NJ | 732-441-2559

Stravino's Italian Store
269 5th St.
Whitehall, PA | 610-432-2551

Vitamia & Sons
206 Harrison Ave.
Lodi, NJ | 800-PASTA-UNO

Woods Seafood
15 Town Wharf
Plymouth, MA | 508-746-0261

Wegmans
3900 Tilghman St.
Allentown, PA | 610-336-7900

Wegmans
5000 Wegmans Dr.
Bethlehem, PA | 610-317-1300

Wegmans
4287 Genesee Valley Plaza
Geneseo, NY | 585-243-9000

Index

A
Advent, 4, 8
Almond Cookies, 32
Anchovies, 13
Anchovies in Garlic Sauce, 13
Anchovy-Stuffed Christmas Peppers, 14
Anisette Cookies, 35
Anisette Liqueur, Homemade, 42
Antipasto, 23

B
Baccala in Dough, 11
Baked Salt Cod, 10
Baked Eel, 16
Beverages, 40
Blood Orange Salad, 28
Broccoli al Dente in Oil and Garlic, 26

C
Calamari, Squid, 17
Campari, Italian Sunset, 40
Candy Cane Cookies, 32
Chestnuts, Drunken, 39
Chestnuts, Roasted, 38
Chestnut Pudding, 39
Chestnuts, 38
Chocolate Pepper Cookie, 31
Cioppino, Seafood Stew, 21
Cuttlefish, 18
Cuttlefish Risotto, 19
Coffee, Sambuca in, 43
Cookie Exchange, 30
Cookie, "S", 33

E
Eel, 15
Eel, Baked, 16
Eel, Fried, 16

F
Feast of Seven Fishes, 8, 9, 20
Fennel, Finocchio, Roasted, 26
Finocchio with Fontina, 27
Finocchio with Parmesan, 27

G
Golden Cadillac, 41
Green Beans and Fresh Tomatoes (Fabiolini Verde Con Pomodori), 26

I
Italian Christmas Eve Punch, 42
Italian Hot Chocolate, 42
Italian Kiss Drink, Rocco's, 41

M
Maniscalco Mind Eraser, The, 41
Marinated Artichokes, 25
Marinated Mushrooms, 25
Midnight Mass, 29

O
Octopus, Polpo, 12
Octopus in Purgatory, 12
Olives, 24

P
Peppers, roasted, 28
Polpo, Octopus, 12

R
Rocco's Italian Kiss Drink, 41

S
"S" Cookies, 33
Salt Cod, 10
Salt Cod, Baked, 11
Salt Cod Salad, 11
Sambuca Toast, 43
Sambuca in Coffee, 43
Seafood Stew, Cioppino, 21
Sister Assunta's Little White
   Wafer Cookies, 33
Smelts, 20
Smelts in Christmas Star
   with Chard, 20
Squid, Calamari, 17
Squid, Fried, 18
Squid in Fresh Tomato Sauce, 17
Stata Buon, 3
Strufoli, 36

T
Tiramisu, 37

V
Vegetables, 23

W
Where to Shop, 47
White Italian Drop Cookies, 34
White Italian Snowballs, 34

Acknowledgments

We would like to thank the following people for their contributions and support in helping to make this cookbook a reality:

Grace Sorrentino Riepensell
Martha Pitarra DeMatio
Ellen Roberts
Margaret Morris
John Hailu
Loretta Diaz
Betsyann Maniscalco Ferraro
Joseph Ferraro
Todd Cucchiara
Rosemarie Hospodore
Chuck Vlasics
Gary Stampone
Uncle John Maniscalco
Frances Curry
Renee Maniscalco
Elda De Annuntis
Susan Weaver
Brother Bernard Seif